SexDrive

STERLING and the distinctive Sterling logo are registered trademarks of
Sterling Publishing Co., Inc.

Library of Congress Cataloging-in-Publication Data

Bronstein, Allen Jake.
 Sex drive : fantasies in flesh and steel / Allen Jake Bronstein.
    p. cm.
 Includes index.
 ISBN-13: 978-1-4027-4922-3
 ISBN-10: 1-4027-4922-8
 1. Photography, Artistic. 2. Photography of automobiles.
 3. Automobiles--Social aspects--United States--Pictorial works. I. Title.

TR650.B695 2007
779'.96292222--dc22

                                        2007020075

10 9 8 7 6 5 4 3 2 1

a ravenous book

Produced by Ravenous, an imprint of Hollan Publishing, Inc.
100 Cummings Center, Suite 125G
Beverly, MA 01915

Published by Sterling Publishing Co., Inc.
387 Park Avenue South, New York, NY 10016

© 2007 by Hollan Publishing, Inc.

Distributed in Canada by Sterling Publishing
c/o Canadian Manda Group, 165 Dufferin Street
Toronto, Ontario, Canada M6K 3H6
Distributed in the United Kingdom by GMC Distribution Services
Castle Place, 166 High Street, Lewes, East Sussex, England BN7 1XU
Distributed in Australia by Capricorn Link (Australia) Pty. Ltd.
P.O. Box 704, Windsor, NSW 2756, Australia

Printed in Singapore

Sterling ISBN-13: 978-1-4027-4922-3
        ISBN-10: 1-4027-4922-8

For information about custom editions, special sales, premium and
corporate purchases, please contact Sterling Special Sales
Department at 800-805-5489 or specialsales@sterlingpub.com.

Photography by Allan Penn
Cover and interior design by Tanya Ross-Hughes/Hotfoot Studio

Hollan Publishing, Inc. would like to thank the Luxe Hotel Sunset Boulevard
for the use of their property to shoot the images on pages 65–67.

Sex Drive

Fantasies in Flesh and Steel

Allen Jake Bronstein

STERLING/RAVENOUS

An imprint of Sterling Publishing Co., Inc.

New York / London
www.sterlingpublishing.com

Contents

INTRODUCTION

Curved fenders, graceful lines, and blinding chrome. Somewhere between the front and rear bumpers, cars awaken a wanton lust. Maybe it's the heat, the speed, the feeling of abandon, escape, or freedom that they give, but something about them makes them the perfect backdrop for the perfect affair. One thing is for sure, though: Long before design was given much thought in other types of consumer goods, cars were given style. They became emblematic of the times from which they came. Tail fins. Suicide doors. Scoops, scallops, and pinstripes. They were thrilling. They were innovative. They were sexy.

Sure, they're made of steel, glass, and chrome, and they run on oil, gas, and water, but cars have become so much more. They are the living embodiment of our hopes and dreams. They are extensions of our personality. They are an opportunity for fantasy fulfillment. They offer the chance of landing the part we've always wanted—becoming the leading man with the sexy co-star of our choosing—in the film that is our life.

It's no mistake we talk about automobiles in much the same way we appreciate a beautiful woman—the perfect curves, the way she moves, the sounds she makes (a whine when we push the limits, a growl when she's got more to give); there's nothing else quite like it on earth. If clothes make the man, cars win the girl. Once you have your dream car, your dream girl is just around the corner, waiting for a lift.

Sex Drive is a celebration of this revered relationship between cars and sex—their intrinsic seductiveness and sensuality. A romp in the bushes is good. One in the backseat of a Lincoln Continental (page 52) is even better—a classy rendezvous in the quintessential lap of luxury. Doing it with the shades up is fun. Doing it with the top down is thrilling and seductively dangerous. Role-play is nice, but there's no better prop than a car from a different era to make that erotic fantasy come true.

Who could've known when Henry Ford was putting every American into an automobile what hot-rodders would eventually make of his Model T (the T-Bucket, page 2)? Likewise, no one could have predicted the awesome lengths to which the massive Cadillacs of the 1960s would stretch (page 40), or the works of art European engineering would bring forth (Ferrari, page 102, Jaguar, page 92). Even less predictable would be the feats that each car's engineering would inspire; the contortions or sordid pleasures consenting adults would one day experience inside of them.

The steamy images of *Sex Drive* will get your blood pumping and your fantasies flowing until you long to turn your own car into a road-going sex machine. But for now, strap yourself in and allow us to take you on this uniquely sensual journey. We know you'll enjoy the ride.

1925 *Ford T-Bucket*

The Ford Model T was produced by the Ford Motor Company from 1908 through 1927. It was the first affordable American automobile (sold for just a few hundred dollars when other cars were priced in the thousands). While it was the first to be built from an assembly line, only eleven were made during the first month of production. By 1914, however, the efficiency of the assembly line had improved, allowing a vehicle to be manufactured in just ninety-three minutes. Still, with thirty shades of black in the palette and a hand crank for a start, there was nothing sexy about it. It wasn't until years later that it got a second life.

From 1945 to 1965, no car on the road was cooler or sexier or got more attention than a tricked-out hot rod. Cars manufactured before 1930, mainly Ford Model Ts and Model As, could be bought for cheap in junkyards or found on blocks in front yards. Of course, the engine, brakes, and steering all had to be replaced before a car could be roadworthy. The roof, hood, windshield, fenders, and bumpers all had to be chopped before it was cool. Add fat wheels for traction, new paint for looks, and what was once worthless tin, a junked piece of car history, was suddenly the kind of showpiece that got more than looks. It was called a T-Bucket, and this asphalt-eating monster got flesh for miles and sex by the pound.

Strictly a "do-it-yourself" job, owning one meant you were a skilled mechanic, welder, and gearhead. It proved you had disposable income and more than a little free time. But the first time you took it out on the road, all that effort more than paid for itself. The big payoff came in the form of heavy breathing, sky-rocketing pulse rates, and overwhelming desire, all of which could often be found in the passenger's seat, just to the driver's right. But while he was in charge of the clutch and throttle, she, as always, was in charge of the ride. Doing it in the T-Bucket meant, more often than not, both parties would be getting out satisfied.

AUTO EROTICA

One of my biggest fantasies has always been having sex on the beach, so when my girlfriend suggested we drive down to the beach for a little nooky, I thought that sounded like a perfect way to make my fantasy come true.

We picked a day that we knew wouldn't be crowded and drove to our favorite spot, which was a little off the beaten path and usually pretty desolate. We parked as close to the shore as we could and climbed into the backseat, both of us dressed in our beach gear, our hearts racing. I kissed her slowly, sensually, and as my tongue entwined with hers, I peeled off her bikini top and let my hands feel their way down. Luckily the backseat of my car was big enough for me to be on top, so after she took off my shorts, I laid her down and slowly entered her, certain that I was experiencing heaven on earth. It was so fantastic—the feel of her, the sensation of the car rocking along with us, the sounds of the waves crashing … It was the best afternoon ever.

—Rich R., 32

"By the mid-1920s, the typical American town was in full sexual bloom. The change came with erotic fashions, literature, and movies, and an unsuspected sexual aid, the automobile."

John Leo

✦ ✦ ✦ ✦

1936 *Auburn Speedster*

Auburn. Duesenberg. Cord. These cars were the epitome of luxury in Hollywood's gilded age. Giant curved fenders, sleek yet graceful lines, open for the world to see. It would be hard to watch one of these behemoths glide by without imagining Marlene Dietrich, face upturned for a photographer's strobe, Fred Astaire dancing his way into women's hearts, and the incredible, rounded proportions of the belles who would glide across the screen in *Gone with the Wind*.

The Auburn Speedster's front end looked like a limo, the tail like a ball gown; the engine was a technological marvel to behold. Each cost nearly ten times that of a sensible automobile, but that was the point. The sound erupting from its tailpipes was unmistakable; the sparkle from its chrome, unavoidable. This was not a car for introverts. There were fewer eyes on the stars who drove them than on the awe-inspiring Auburn Speedsters that cruised through Hollywood.

In 1936, in the midst of the Depression, the Auburn Supercharged Boat-Tail Speedster was priced at $2,245, almost ten times the price of a Model A Ford. Despite the cost, their stunning looks, speed, and opulence made these cars very popular with the Hollywood set. Errol Flynn, Clark Gable, Gary Cooper, James Cagney, and Marlene Dietrich are just a

few of the stars who owned one of these beautiful automobiles.

Owning one meant you were a part of the elite. It gave you entrée into the finest clubs and most exclusive parties. But more important, it allowed access into the lacy underthings of women who might not normally allow such behavior. That is, until they admired the suggestive pipes snaking their way through the hood, felt the rumble, and were pressed into their seats by the thrust that only a car able to achieve 100 mph was capable of—one of the few cars that could make such a claim at the time. Then, and only then, did they throw caution to the wind.

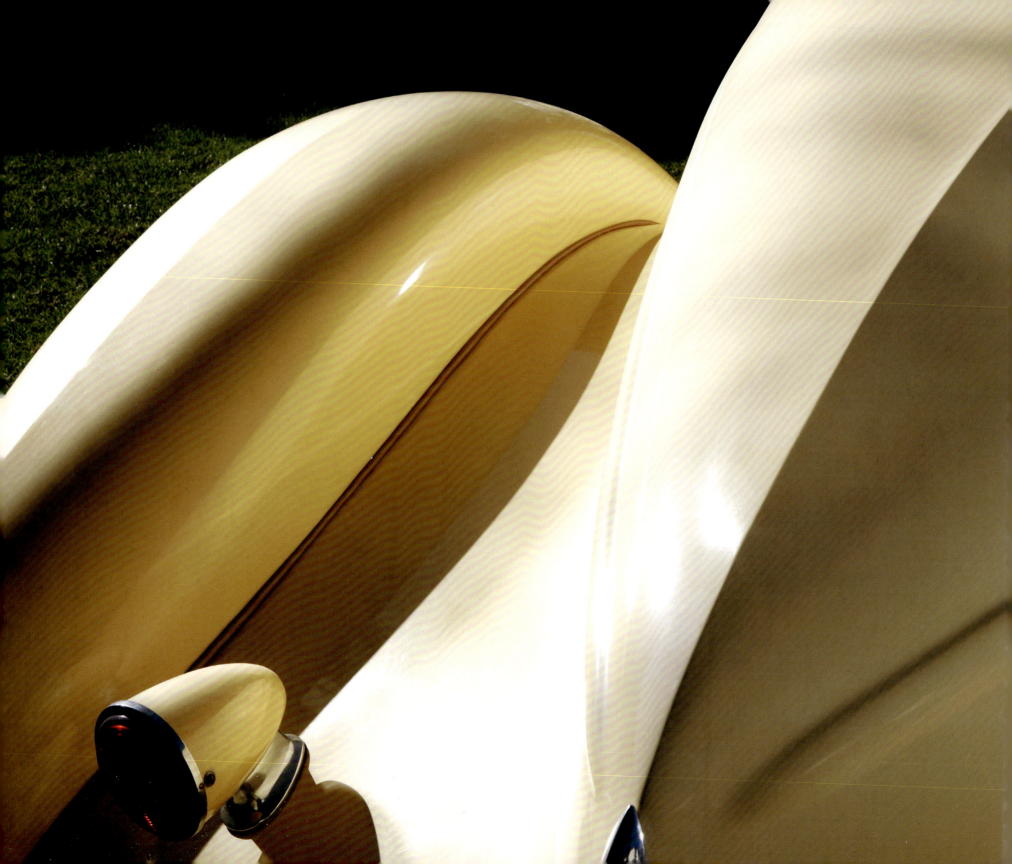

> **"Sex is an emotion in motion."**
> *Mae West*
>
> ✦ ✦ ✦ ✦

AUTO EROTICA

Nowadays too much emphasis is put on going "all the way." Sure, you have a couple dates and share a couple kisses, but after that, it's usually wham, bam, thank you ma'am—right into the sack. So one night my boyfriend and I drove to a nearby makeout spot and started playing the game of "Everything But." We necked and groped like horny teenagers, letting our hands and lips do the talking as we steamed up the windows. I dug my hands into his hair as I teased him with my lips on his. He attempted to stick his hand under my sweater and I swatted it away, and that almost made it hotter—the fact that we set a ground rule not to go farther than second base. The more passionate our kissing and groping, the harder it was to keep from hopping in the backseat. We even had a cop stop by to break it all up! It was perfect.

—Annie K., 36

1946 *Ford Woodie*

Endless summers, surfboards, bikini-clad Gidgets dancing by the bonfire while Beach Boys tunes echo in their minds—the Woodie Wagon (regardless of year, make, or model) holds a special place in seaside culture. Fans have their favorites, but in the end, it's all about popping the wood—the more of it, the better. Why, you ask? The answer is simple: Wood evokes warmth. Warmth means summer. Summer means beaches. Beaches mean surf and skin. Wet skin. Moist, muscular, browned-to-perfection skin. All of it in motion, and very little of it covered. It's enough to fuel daydreams about sitting behind the wheel of a classic like the 1946 Ford Super Deluxe (shown here) and enjoying your own beachside rendezvous.

Its history dates all the way back to the very beginning of production cars. Back then, if you wanted extra interior space or a larger body, you had to somehow tack it onto the frame yourself. Until the late '30s, most cars and trucks used wood in the construction of the body, though most, if not all, was covered to the outside observer in steel. But steel was expensive and hard to work with, and welders were hard to come by, so those desperate to expand used wood. It was easier to use, rigid, cheap, and reliable. No one cared that it was tantamount to wearing underwear outside your clothes; these cars were about function.

The original Woodies were the first "station wagons," so called because, at the time, almost everyone traveled by train, if they traveled at all. The old Fords were specially modified to carry passengers and their giant trunks to and from train stations. The term stuck and has been used ever since to denote any car with extra space for passengers and luggage.

Henry Ford came up with quite a few innovations that revolutionized auto manufacturing. He was always looking for ways to cut manufacturing costs, and, in 1929, he opened his own lumber mill in Iron Mountain, Michigan, to mill the wood used in the construction of Ford bodies. He broke further ground by being the first manufacturer to offer Woodie bodies as a regular catalog item.

By the mid–'40s, wood construction costs surpassed those of metal, and the cars that now came from the factory covered in wood became toys for the rich. It wasn't until decades later, when surfers started picking them up secondhand at bargain prices, that the name "Woodie" was born.

Today, the important thing is that it's got space enough that girls can jump in the

back and change from bikinis to jeans (and from girls to women if they're kind enough to invite the boys along) without exposing tan lines to passersby outside. It's still about function, but it's also about friction. Everyone on the beach knows that if a Woodie's a-rockin', you don't come a-knockin'. Some do more than rock, though; they bang. Car buffs will tell you it's because of their ultra-springy suspensions, others swear . . . well, let's just say, according to legend, some of the greatest surfers don't only hang ten on the waves.

AUTO EROTICA

I'll be honest—I never learned how to drive. I never saw the point. I'd rather read or do crosswords on the bus than sit in a car in traffic and have to pay attention to the road.

Since I didn't have my license, my boyfriend always drove us when we went somewhere together. We were on a romantic getaway in Southern California, when—for seemingly no reason—we came to a dead stop on the freeway for what felt like forever. He started getting agitated, so I decided to ease his stress. I leaned over and whispered in his ear that traffic jams could be fun, then let my tongue trace its way down his neck to his collarbone as I unzipped his pants. I took a quick peek around and gave silent thanks for tinted windows as I went down on him. Once I got him worked up enough, I shimmied out of my pants and carefully crawled into his lap, lowering myself down on him. I planted my feet on the dashboard on either side of the steering wheel, and used the ceiling and the middle console for leverage. I have no idea how he managed, but traffic started moving a little before we were done, and he was somehow able to drive while he was bringing me to ecstasy! Now whenever he gets into the car, he prays for a traffic jam!

—Monica G., 26

ON CAR SEX . . .

THE LOWDOWN
There's something sexy about that urgency—that voice in your head that tells you that you have to have this person NOW. When desire hits you to the extent that you just can't wait to get to a bedroom, it can make for some really explosive sex. Plus, cars are hot!

TIPS AND TECHNIQUES
Different bodies and different cars will produce different results. A compact car will likely be hard for him to maneuver in, but that can make your tryst all the more creative.

—Carly Milne, editor of *Naked Ambition* and contributor to *Hooking Up: You'll Never Make Love in This Town Again*

"Kids in cars cause accidents. Accidents in cars cause kids."

Unknown

♦ ♦ ♦ ♦

1949 *Mercury Coupe*

The war had recently ended, but things still looked bleak. Gray. Uninspired. Memories of violence and destruction still hung heavy in the air. The country was eager to return to some kind of normalcy. So in April 1948, three years after the big bombs dropped, when a new Mercury rolled off the line, people took notice. This was, after all, the first major restyling of a vehicle since Pearl Harbor had been attacked.

It was lower, wider, and longer than anything that had come before. There were fade-away fenders, suicide doors for the sedans, a massive grille, and giant parking lights. It was distinctive, it was revolutionary, it was unique—and yet, it wasn't nearly enough. Not by a long shot.

Within minutes of its arrival, it was leapt on by customizers. Chrome was removed. Tops were chopped. Side spears were tacked on. Aftermarket engines were added. Suspensions were lowered. What had been just a car was suddenly a statement about one's personality, a chance to express oneself. It was an explosion of a different sort.

While women spent their time at the salon sitting beneath giant hairdryers, men were sliding under the "leadsleds" (so called for the extensive lead work that was needed to fill the holes left in the body once the factory parts were pulled). While the girls painted

their nails, the cars were pinstriped and candy-coated. Dresses were hemmed. Fenders extended. The women dolled up. The cars decked out. And it all came together in the parking lots and on the straightaways. This was the new war, a war in which cars competed for pride, raced for pink slips, and could somehow let even the greasiest gearhead walk away with the ultimate trophy: The girl of his dreams and the chance to show her the work yet to be done in the backseat.

The definitive car of an era, the '49 Mercury, was featured in a number of movies and television shows. In the original *Batman* TV series, Bruce Wayne drove the convertible top-down, while his crime-fighting alter ego drove it top-up. Pharaoh's gang drove a custom Merc in *American Graffiti*. No one made more of an impact, though, than when James Dean drove his Mercury,

dechromed, in *Rebel Without a Cause*. Sadly, the movie's premiere was at New York's Astor Theatre in October 1955, one month after Dean's death. But rolled-up sleeves, chopped-up cars, and teenage angst never looked so good. The image of Dean racing that Merc chop would live forever.

AUTO EROTICA

My husband was big into road trips, and I never was. I never had an issue with the drive or what kind of car we were driving so much as how long the drive took. He never wanted to go anywhere that was a quick jaunt—it always had to be an eleven-hour trip. So when he told me he had a special treat for me on our next road trip to make it easier on me, I have to admit I was both interested and skeptical. What could he possibly have that could make me enjoy a road trip? I got my answer right around the two-hour mark. He told me to open the glove compartment, and there, in a little white box, was a vibrator meant to plug into the lighter outlet that most older cars have. I knew exactly what he expected, so I plugged it in and went to work. First, I took care of myself, and it felt so good! Then, I put on a little bit of a show for him to get him going. Finally, I pulled out all the stops and got naughty. I suggestively unbuttoned my blouse and slipped the fingers on my free hand into his mouth as I pleasured myself with the other hand and talked so dirty you'd have thought I was channeling *Penthouse* Letters. I knew I'd made the best use out of his little gift for me when we never made it to our destination, choosing instead to have hot and dirty sex in a roadside hotel all weekend!

—Tara H., 32

ON CAR SEX . . .

THE LOWDOWN

Between memories of first kisses, first touches, and first-time sex for so many people, the car represents a naughty playground where young lovers were able to get away with all of those things they weren't supposed to be doing.

TIPS AND TECHNIQUES

I wouldn't recommend lying down across the backseat since this is likely to be very uncomfortable and your movement is rather restricted. Sitting positions are best suited for car sex, unless you have the option of spreading out in the back of your SUV or pickup.

—Yvonne K. Fulbright, Ph.D., author of *Touch Me There! A Hands-on Guide to Your Orgasmic Hot Spots* and *Pleasuring*

"There is nothing wrong with making love with the light on. Just make sure the car door is closed."

George Burns

✦ ✦ ✦ ✦

1954 *GMC Pickup*

Men in trucks are doers, not talkers. They are men of action, men who know the value of a hard day's work. They are men who are good with their oversized, calloused hands. Men who don't mind getting dirty, if that's what it takes to get the job done right. Men who break a sweat over the course of a day and make women sweat over the course of a night. Sure, women want to marry white-collar guys with solid 401(k) and life insurance policies. But women want to be taken by blue-collar men with dirt under their fingernails and the occasional hard-earned bruise. Of course, men in vintage trucks are a slightly different breed.

True, all of the above still applies. Men in vintage trucks are men who wear jeans. Men who know their way around a power tool, a construction site, and a woman's body. But those jeans probably cost a little extra, and fit a little better. That construction site? It's probably their own dream home they're building. And they way they handle women? They're a bit rough around the edges, but they also know the value of a tender touch. Men in vintage trucks are real men. But they are real men of style.

So what kind of woman goes for a man in a vintage '54 GMC pickup (like the one pictured)? What kind of woman *doesn't*? Even city gals dream of being pushed up against a

giant fender, being bent over a muddy flatbed, or kneeling in front of a well-worn grille from time to time. And even city boys, perhaps *especially city boys*, dream of being the ones to do it to them. Step one is buying the hardware.

In 1901, Max Grabowsky established the Rapid Motor Vehicle Company with the intention of developing some of the world's first commercial-grade trucks. Though extremely rugged, with just a one-cylinder engine under the hood, most were underpowered. Still, just eight years later, General Motors bought the company, and in 1912 the first GMC truck was ready for public consumption. The vehicles made their debut at that year's New York Auto Show, where they were instantly embraced.

The ol' '54 featured the first factory-installed turn signal to be incorporated into the steering column, but it didn't end there; GMC trucks have a long history of record-setting. In 1916, one made the cross-country trek from Seattle to New York in a record-breaking thirty days. Ten years later, yet another record was smashed when a two-ton GMC was driven the other way, from New York to San Francisco, in just over five days.

> "There are two things no man will admit he cannot do well: drive and make love."
>
> *Stirling Moss*

♦ ♦ ♦ ♦

AUTO EROTICA

During a cross-country road trip with my girlfriend, I came up with the idea of playing a sort of dirty version of "I Spy"—we had to spot things that were sexual in nature and tell each other a story about it. We were in the middle of Utah, or maybe it was Colorado, when I spotted a cowboy on a horse. I told her a story about using a riding crop lightly on her, teasing and tickling her most sensitive areas. She saw a couple kissing passionately outside of a rest stop and wove a tale about how the two of them were so overcome by their desire for each other that they had to stop somewhere so they could get their hands on each other. Both of us were getting so hot and bothered that when I spotted a seedy motel up the road, I pulled in, parked in an empty spot, and took her right then and there. There were no words, and we barely took any time to undress . . . I didn't even turn off the ignition! From that moment on, we never had another boring road trip.

—Ross W., 39

1958 *Chevrolet Corvette*

At a time when most Americans would live a complete life within a two-hundred-mile radius from where they were born, the GIs returning home from World War II were bringing back more than simply stories and scars. Having seen the world, they realized they'd yet to see beyond their own backyards. They had wanderlust. But perhaps more important, some of them had cars. Small ones. Two-seaters. Imported, inexpensive roadsters that seemed to celebrate the pavement like never before. Something had to be done. It was Chevrolet that would answer the call.

Roadside diners, endless highways, sea to shining sea—there was exploring to be done. What began as a simple love affair with the road, a love affair with America, would soon build into a love affair with the Corvette, the first all-American sports car built by an all-American car manufacturer right here in the good old U.S. of A. Earlier models had been criticized for being crude and lacking the refinement of European sports cars, but by '58 (pictured), they'd gotten the formula right: a fiberglass body, four headlights, pounds of chrome, the mouth, the scoops, the colors, the curves, and an elegantly simple engine and gearbox that delivered so much power they had to install a passenger side grab rail in the dashboard that would later be dubbed a "sissy bar."

ON CAR SEX . . .

THE LOWDOWN

Sex in cars? Of course! Cars are very sexy. The sexy image is what sells cars, particularly the more expensive ones. Being associated with that image, combined with the naughtiness of having sex out of the bedroom, amps up the juices.

TIPS AND TECHNIQUES

For one thing, make sure the alarm is off, since rocking can trigger a siren you won't want to hear. Secondly, if you have an encounter on the hood, make sure you haven't just run the engine, otherwise you'll have more heat than you expected.

—Joel D. Block, Ph.D., psychologist, sex therapist, and author of *The Art of the Quickie*

It was instant nostalgia. The shapes would become classics. The design, an icon. And the days spent bounding over the hillsides, picnicking at pit stops, and pulling into and out of inns and motels, exploring with the perfect companion in the passenger seat, legendary.

Of course, their hands wandered, too. They weren't just exploring the geography with their companions; her geography begged to be charted as well. In the driver's seat, heart rates went up. In the passenger's seat, even prudes went down. And before they knew it, the formal '50s gave way to the free-love '60s. The rest, as they say, is history.

In Chevrolet's tiny, underdog Corvette division, they knew a good idea could come from just about anywhere. In fact, the name, drawn from the small, fast "Corvette class" warships, was dreamt up by Myron Scott, Chevrolet's chief photographer. Meanwhile, the bowtie logo, inspired by a wallpaper pattern in a Paris hotel, was designed by Robert Bartholomew, an interior designer at Chevrolet in 1953.

The original emblem, featuring crossed American and checkered flags, had to be changed to contain a black-and-white

AUTO EROTICA

Guys in sports cars turn me on—I can't help it. I don't know if it's their self-assured attitude or the car itself that does it for me, or maybe it's the combination of the two. Whatever it is, it gets me going every time.

One afternoon I was sitting at an outdoor café watching the world go by, and this guy pulled up in a really cool convertible. On his way out of the café, he noticed me staring at his car and asked me if I wanted a ride. I couldn't resist. So I hopped in the passenger seat and off we went, zipping in and out of traffic. When he grabbed my hand and put it on the gear shift, I knew I wanted him. We stopped for a breather and got out of the car, and I walked around front, leaning back against the hood. When he joined me, he leaned in and kissed me, sending shivers all the way down to my toes, even though the hood was still hot from our speedy drive. He leaned me back over the hood and I curled my legs around his waist, murmuring with pleasure as he nibbled my neck. Just as things were starting to get interesting, some people rounded the corner and started hooting and hollering. We laughed and he drove me home. Though I never heard from him again, I never lost my soft spot for sports-car guys.

checkered flag, a red Chevrolet bowtie, and the fleur-de-lis, as it is against U.S. law to use an American flag on any product to be trademarked.

Known as "double-o-three" amongst Corvette historians (for its serial number, E53F001003), the third 'Vette to roll off the line in '53 is thought to be the oldest known surviving production Corvette. In 2006, this legendary auto fetched an unheard-of $1 million at auction.

"The true man wants two things: danger and play. For that reason he wants woman, as the most dangerous plaything."

Friedrich Nietzche

◆ ◆ ◆ ◆

1958 *Rolls Royce Phantom V*

Rolls Royce. The very cream of the crop. If you have to ask, not only can you probably not afford it, you're probably not a captain of industry, rock star, title-holding royal, or oil-rich sheik. You'll never know what it's like to have the world at your fingertips, supermodels on speed-dial, a private jet waiting on the runway, an entourage to cater to your every whim, or estates at the ready worldwide.

The Phantom V (shown) is the very best of the best. It measured a staggering nineteen feet long and displaced close to two and a half tons, yet its V8 was capable of speeds of more than 120 miles per hour. It had an ultra-low gear that allowed it to move at an even and steady pace, just a hair faster than a walk, so people could get a good look during "official functions." Only 516 were built, each with a custom interior completely tailored to its owner's every desire. It was only the '50s, but car phones weren't out of reach. Neither were in-car refrigerators, televisions, or custom stereos and seating configurations. Even beds could be installed (as was the case on John Lennon's, which also bore a world famous psychedelic paint job). Suicide doors, aftermarket bulletproofing, and, of course, that unmistakable winged woman on the hood presiding over it all.

On March 15, 1906, the company was formed when Frederick Henry Royce, an electrical and mechanical business owner who'd built a car called a Royce in 1904, agreed to a deal with Charles Stewart Rolls at the Midland Hotel in Manchester, England. Royce would manufacture cars to be sold exclusively by Rolls. When a last-minute clause was added to the contract stipulating the cars would be called Rolls-Royce, history was made.

First you get the money, then you get the power, then you get the women. Tony Montana, who expressed this sentiment in *Scarface*, was chauffeured around in a Rolls once he'd made his fortune. It was the car that Randolph and Mortimer Duke watched the stock market from in *Trading Places*. It also ferried more British royals, kings, queens, princes, and princesses than any other auto on earth—and some British pop royalty as well. John Lennon's V had to be sold at auction when the Cooper-Hewitt Museum could no longer afford the insurance required to display it for the public. Fetching over $2.2 million, the car remains to this day one of the most valuable pieces of music memorabilia in the world.

If these cars could talk, they would no doubt tell tales of wealthy industrialists seducing the mistresses they kept on the side; bored matrons taking out their frustrations on the gardener and

pool boy, sometimes at the same time; Hollywood producers picking up wannabe starlets, only to submit them to the casting couch on the way to the set and drop them off again before they get there. Tickles, teases, grinding, and gold diggers. Hot breath, high couture, panting, panties, parties, money, and moaning, and all of it hidden from sight behind tinted windows. If money is the ultimate aphrodisiac, a Rolls is the icing on the cake, the lube that greases the wheels and primes the pistons. Everyone who's anyone knows it. And anyone less is hardly worth talking to. At least for someone of your stature.

AUTO EROTICA

Sex in a car was always something I wanted to experience. So when I surprised my wife with a night on the town in celebration of our anniversary, she knew the limo ride was as much a gift for me as it was for her.

We wasted no time getting down to business. Though I was in my tux and she was in an elegant gown, she quickly but carefully undid my tie and peeled off my jacket as I slid my hands up the outsides of her legs, sliding her dress upward as I went. I'd told the driver that I wanted to do a drive around the city before we reached our first destination, so that, coupled with the space we had to work with, meant we were able to transition from position to position without any issue—me on top, her on top, me taking her from behind, her sitting on my lap. By the time we made it to the restaurant, we were nearly too tired to go in, but we composed ourselves and momentarily left our mobile love nest to refuel. As we exited, the driver gave me a wink. Knowing he knew what was going on made the experience that much hotter.

—Martin W., 37

"In love, somehow, a man's heart is always either exceeding the speed limit or getting parked in the wrong place."

Helen Rowland

✦ ✦ ✦ ✦

1960 *Cadillac Convertible*

With a distance of eighteen feet, nine inches from chromed-out bumper to chromed-out bumper, the 1960 Cadillac was as big as a whale. It didn't drive down streets, it occupied them. Stand it on end and it was nearly two stories tall. Hell, even the fender skirts measured a staggering thirty-seven inches long. But as most women will attest, it's not the size of the boat, but the motion in the ocean that counts. In that category, as in most, the 1960 Caddy made waves. Big ones.

Previous models had been the very pinnacle of excess, but their features were minimal by comparison. Cadillac's tail fins appeared in 1948 and by '59 they'd nearly doubled in size. The fins weren't the only part of the vehicle that was engorged: The wheelbase swelled to 130 inches and the 390-cubic-inch V8 pumped out 325 horsepower. It needed every inch of available thrust to make the buxom 4,850-pound figure move. Sure, the gas tank held twenty-eight gallons, but it wouldn't get you very far.

But Caddys have never been about *when* you get there, rather about *how* you get there. It's all about the ride. And riding in one of these beauties meant you were riding in style.

Cadillac has always been a trailblazer. In 1910 it was the first manufacturer to release cars with a fully enclosed cab as factory equipment; the first to offer an internal

"I think that for some reason when a man is driving down that freeway of love, the woman he's with is like an exit, but he doesn't want to get off there. He wants to keep driving."

Jerry Seinfeld

✦ ✦ ✦ ✦

combustion engine with an electric start, as opposed to a crank (1911—it was marketed as a convenience for female drivers); and the first manufacturer to utilize the skills of a designer instead of an engineer to produce a car's body (1927).

In 1932, Cadillac was in a slump. In fact, the whole brand was set to be mothballed. It probably would have fallen into extinction if not for an eleventh-hour plea from Cadillac president Nicholas Dreystadt to the GM board of directors. Racism was nothing worth batting an eyelash at in the '30s, but when Dreystadt heard a rumor that African-American boxer Joe Louis had to send a white emissary to the lot to make a purchase, he knew he had a problem. In a bold move, Dreystadt proposed directing more advertising to African-American clientele. The board gave Dreystadt a year and a half to show results. Not only did Cadillac regain profitability, it was the only American automobile manufacturer to remain profitable during the Great Depression.

The '60 model was scaled back ever so slightly, mainly around the now-slimmer fins and fenders, resulting in a Cadillac that emanated an undisputable cool that had been lacking in past models. Elvis gave them as gifts. "Life, liberty, and the pursuit" was the slogan, but owning one proved you weren't chasing the dream—you already held the keys. To this day, the car has a swagger that simply can't be ignored. It exudes confidence. It's not the wallflower, it's the showboat, a peacock that demands attention. Pulling up to a woman's bumper in one could easily lead to pulling up to her bumper inside of one. But there's only so much the car can do; if you're really looking to impress, the rest is on you. Work it hard.

AUTO EROTICA

I was too young to experience the initial drive-in movie craze, but when one reopened near my home, I made my boyfriend swear that he would take me, even though he kept complaining that a movie theatre was much more fun. I promised him we'd have plenty of fun at the drive-in, so he finally agreed.

When we got there, I asked him to go to the concession stand and get us popcorn and drinks while I made the backseat comfortable for us. I dropped the front seats forward, laid out some blankets and pillows, and by the time he got back to the car, he discovered me in the backseat wearing only my lingerie and a smile. He hopped in the backseat with me and put down our snacks so he could kiss and caress me. We made love passionately, but quietly, until the action picked up in the movie, and then I had no qualms about moaning my appreciation. Now he wants to go to the drive-in all the time!

—Sherry C., 25

1960 *Porsche 356 Cabriolet*

Long before Gordon Gekko and his hedge-fund cowboys branded Porsche the ultimate status symbol, before the power ties and power lunches, before the 911 became the symbol of conspicuous consumption it is today, the 356, the first car ever to bear the Porsche name, was simply a fun car. A car without pretension. A souped-up Volkswagen built for a driver who embraced every day as his last, every minute as another chance at freedom, and every second as a lifetime to savor.

Porsche has always believed in evolution, not model years. While the competition put out a new variation of an old car every twelve months, at Porsche, they only fixed the problems they found. Naturally, the product improved incrementally over time. Sure, aluminum was replaced with steel, disc brakes were added, and the engine tweaked some, but generally, little was changed over the course of the seventeen years the 356 was rolling off production lines. And why should it? The Mona Lisa gets restored, not remodeled. Why tamper with perfection?

Trends come and go, and over the years the look of those buckled in no doubt evolved—from the elbow-patch-wearing WASPs of the '40s with their pink-and-pearls playthings beside them to the bead-wearing rock stars of the '60s enjoying the show as the

groupies they'd packed in flashed fellow motorists. Some fashions are never out of style: To this day, the 356 remains a sexy auto that demands a certain kind of driver. The rear-mounted engine takes a deft touch to control in a turn. The removable windshield demands a free spirit to enjoy. It's a car for a purist who wants nothing more than to get behind the wheel and go. It's for the type who appreciates a car capable of turning a trip around the block into an outing, a ride around town into an event, and a simple road trip into a love affair.

True, some find the Wall Street bonuses that purchase Porsches today sexy, but long before that, these open-top beauties were powering lovers up and down Laurel Canyon, escorting romantics to Napa Valley, and cannonballing couples to Palm Springs. Could anything be more romantic?

The 356 has more movie credits than Robert De Niro. It can be seen in *48 Hours, Doc Hollywood, Faster, Pussycat! Kill! Kill!, Point Break, Top Gun, Shampoo, The Return of the Dragon, The Kid, Hollywood Knights,* and *K2*—and the list goes on and on. Discerning fans will even recognize it from *Willy Wonka & the Chocolate Factory*; Charlie uncovers his golden ticket while standing in front of one. But no onscreen appearance is more enjoyable than the car's starring ride in 1968's *Bullitt*. The movie, starring Steve McQueen, is known for its goofs: People's clothes change from scene to scene. Crew members can be spotted in the background. You can even count the staggering number of hubcaps the Bullitt and his 356 lose during what is arguably the greatest car chase ever committed to film.

The 356 has long been a favorite of celebrities like McQueen, who not only owned a 356, 908, and 917, but was also known to

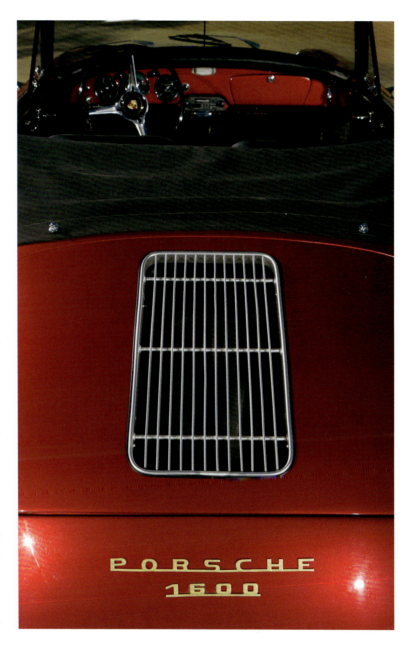

race Porsche prototypes in his downtime. Janis Joplin had her 356 painted with psychedelic swirls by Dave Richards to match her public persona. And Jerry Seinfeld, known to have amassed one of the largest private Porsche collections in the world, went so far as to build a million-dollar parking garage on Manhattan's Upper West Side to house his favorites.

AUTO EROTICA

I don't think there's a man alive who wouldn't want to combine his two greatest passions—sex and cars. So when I finally had the chance to get it on in a sports car with my girlfriend, I wasn't going to let a little thing like lack of space get in my way. I drove us to one of the lookout points on Mulholland Drive. With the shining lights of the valley below us, we started things in the front seat. Kissing was awesome—petting was even better—but as we started trying to undress each other we became aware of the limitations of my vehicle. Bucket seats were comfortable enough for driving, but for moving around when trying to get naked? Not so much. Finally, I took her outside, where I peeled her pants off and laid her down on the hood. Simply put, it was an incredible experience. We could still feel the heat from the engine as we made love! Days later I noticed a scratch on the hood from where she'd inadvertently dug her heel in, but I couldn't bring myself to get it fixed—every time I saw it, it put a smile on my face.

—Perry C., 29

"Lust of power burns more fiercely than all the passions combined."

Irish Blessing

❖ ❖ ❖ ❖

1961 *Lincoln Continental*

The lines were clean, uncluttered. The proportions well tailored, perfect. There was little to no extraneous detail or decoration, no two-tone paint, no overblown chrome, no sharp styling cues to accentuate its beauty. Tasteful. And yet, locked between its flat side panels and inset bumpers, somewhere between simplicity and elegant, the beauty was there. Is it any surprise this was the official vehicle chosen to ferry John F. Kennedy and wife Jacqueline—the very definitions of poise, composure, and grace—during their Camelot years in the White House?

In a way, it's amazing there ever *was* a 1961 Lincoln. Robert S. McNamara—yes, *that* Robert S. McNamara—then head of operations for the Ford Motor Company, wanted to drop the line, as previous incarnations had lost the company upward of $1,000 per unit. But it was a design proposal for a new Thunderbird that eventually set the 1961 Lincoln in motion. The mock-up was "too nice" for a Thunderbird, so McNamara, not wanting to scrap it, decided it should become the new Continental, only it would have to be stretched to Lincoln length without losing its carefully refined proportions. It would also have to come in both hardtop and ragtop models. As for the suicide doors—the front-opening rear doors that would come to define it—incredibly, they were purely a practical decision.

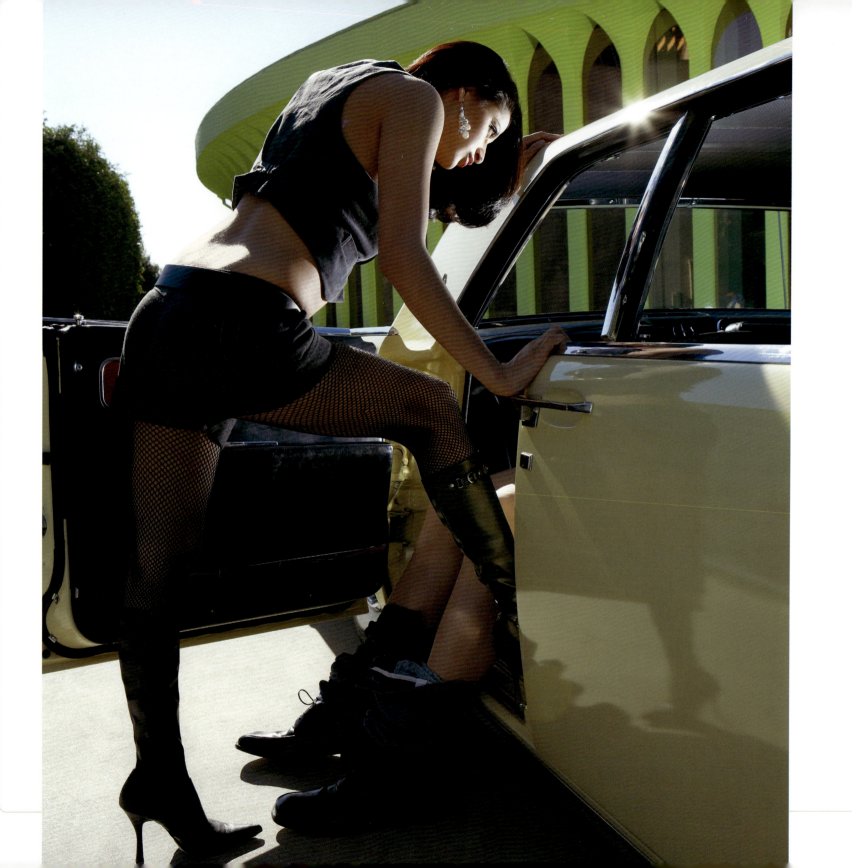

There simply was not enough structural strength to front-hang the heavy rear doors in the convertible model.

Originally developed for Edsel Ford's Florida vacation in March of '39, neither the company, nor Ford himself, had any real intention of mass-producing and marketing the vehicle to the general public. However, following the car's delivery to the sunshine state, reaction was so positive among Ford's society friends that the chairman sent a telegram back to the factory. The message was simple: Build more! Lincoln craftsmen and engineers immediately set about the task, fabricating models in both convertible and sedan form.

The Continental name returned in '55. Cars built under the banner were some of the most expensive available for purchase throughout the end of the decade. Only 3,000 were sold in total, but they went almost exclusively to the world's most famous and/or richest men, including Henry Kissinger, Elvis Presley, the Shah of Iran, and Nelson Rockefeller.

If anything could be learned from this gorgeous car and those who inhabited it, it's that there's an elegance to simplicity. Luxury doesn't have to be ostentatious. Incredible autos can come without egos. And sometimes, just sometimes, sexier roadside attractions can be seen taking place in the backseat than through the front windshield. For the chauffeurs forced to drive this divider-free limo, the real challenge was to resist adjusting the mirror for a better view of the landscape in the rear compartment.

"Any man who can drive safely while kissing a pretty girl is simply not giving the kiss the attention it deserves."

Albert Einstein

♦ ♦ ♦ ♦

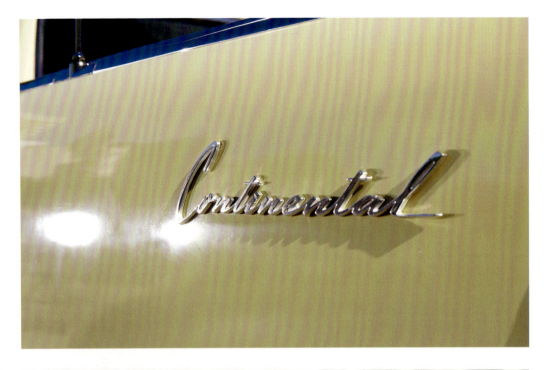

AUTO EROTICA

I was in a particularly frisky mood as my boyfriend drove us to his parents' place. He was nervous, so I teased my fingers down his neck and inside his shirt, tracing his ear with my tongue, anything to try and get him to release some tension. Nothing seemed to be working, so finally I told him to pull into an empty parking lot. When he turned off the ignition, I leaned over and undid his jeans, told him to relax, and went down on him, my fingers continuing to tease him along with my tongue. I could feel his stress melting away as he started moving his hips against me, and even though I had my heel stuck in the door handle and the gear shift in my stomach, I didn't care. Giving him pleasure was all that was on my mind, and from the looks of things, he was definitely enjoying himself! When he finished, he kissed me passionately and thanked me, and then looked at his watch. We were late! He promised he'd make it up to me on the ride home, and he did . . . but that's a story for another time.

—Leslie B., 31

1965 *Shelby Cobra*

Statistically speaking, your odds of ever spotting what appears to be a Shelby Cobra on the street are rather slim. Your odds of seeing an authentic one, however, practically nonexistent. Simply put, as rare as it is, the Cobra is the most copied, duplicated, replicated, and cloned car on the face of the earth. But just like Jack Nicholson's oft-imitated smile, there is nothing quite as sexy as an original. To this day, Cobras have no substitute, equal, or parallel.

Its story starts with a letter, mailed from Carroll Shelby, a noted Texas race car driver, to AC Cars of England, dated September 1961. Shelby was looking for a tiny body into which he could force the largest V8 he could find. AC, having fallen on hard times, was more than happy to oblige, and within hours of the engineless body's stateside arrival, Shelby had it up and running. It didn't take much more than a single test drive to realize he'd created something special. Ford, wanting a car that could compete against the Corvette, did everything it could to help.

The car was fast: 180 mph when tuned for the track. It broke records. Its fat rear tires, giant radiator opening, and utter disregard for the comfort a roof could provide turned heads. Yet over the course of six years and three models (the Mark I, Mark II, and Mark III), fewer than one thousand were assembled by the AC-Shelby partnership.

Toward the end, as the market fell out for Cobras, thirty-one unsold competition cars were detuned and made roadworthy. These units were dubbed S/C, for semi-competition. Today they are considered the rarest and the most valuable of the models and can easily sell in excess of $1.5 million.

At the time, Corvette was the car to beat on racetracks worldwide. Shelby wanted his Cobra to be the new forerunner, and with this singular goal in place, it was in fact his roadster that amassed the most checkered flags in the years following its release. By some accounts, the car may have even been too fast. One was given to Shelby's close friend Bill Cosby, but the

> ## "Is there a speed limit on love?"
>
> *Loesje*
>
> ✦ ✦ ✦ ✦

comedian was forced to give it up, as he kept losing control of it. Its next owner had even less luck when the same issue sent it careening off a cliff.

In addition to the Cobra and the special-edition Mustang for which he is best known, Shelby also helped develop and style the Viper super-car in the late 1990s. The original model was kept by Carroll Shelby himself over the years as a personal car. In January 2007 it was auctioned at the Barrett-Jackson Collector Car Auction in Scottsdale, Arizona, where it fetched a staggering $5.5 million.

To this day, kits and conversions far outnumber the actual vehicle that inspired them. Its styling can be seen in Mazda's Miata; its attitude in Porsche's Boxster. But its panty-soaking, hard-on forging, pressure-cooking sex appeal is as yet unrivaled. It would seem you're more likely to make love to a supermodel than to make love in this supermodel. As for which you should choose if given the option? The answer is obvious. Hell, even the catwalkers themselves probably lust after them—the smarter ones anyway. Eat your cake and have it, too. Then eat as much of the other stuff as you like on the ride home.

AUTO EROTICA

Nothing perks up a lonely drive quite like a little "car flirting" with your fellow drivers. Once I spotted a hot blonde driving a few lanes away from me, so I made an effort to pull up next to her and get her attention. She noticed me and smiled back, and we started playing a little game of cat and mouse. She'd speed up and pretend to try and lose me, and I'd do the same. She'd wink and blow kisses, and I'd motion for her to pull off at the next exit. Finally she did, and I followed her until she parked. I parked right behind her and met her in between my car and hers, where I bent her backward over her trunk and kissed her with everything I had in me. She dug her hands in my hair and hung on around my neck, kicking her feet up and planting her heels on the bumper of my car as my hands searched under her shirt and her hands pulled at the waistband of my pants. Before things got too heated and we were cited for indecent exposure, she gave me her number and asked me to call her. I did, and we more than finished what we started . . . I made her my wife!

—Adam G., 33

1965 *Chevrolet Corvette Stingray*

Some cars make you want to make love—gently caress, blow on moistened skin, tease, tickle, and tingle. The Stingray was not that car. It begged men to be predators, hunting for women—their prey. Hair-pulling, unbridled aggression, rough and tumble, the kind of encounter that leaves marks on both bodies and minds. This wasn't the kind of sex married couples enjoy after a carefully scheduled night out. It was the break-up and make-up sex that comes out of nowhere, strikes with a fury, and somehow fixes everything while you tear each other apart. Sometimes it doesn't matter what sparks the inferno, just as long as the flame keeps burning.

But what lead the '57 "diner Corvette" to evolve into the sleek, intimidating predator it would grow up to be just seven years later? Some think that designer Bill Mitchell was doing his best to recreate Jaguar's E-Type here on American soil. Maybe it had something to do with the wildlife he saw while deep-sea fishing. Wherever the spark originated that led him to take an otherwise docile, rounded, two-tone car, and shave it down to a sliver, dress it up with side exhaust pipes, and slash into it with menacing vents that looked like gills, it was nothing short of genius. And what it would inspire in others was a lust second to none.

So what exactly inspires someone to bite a lover somewhere new? Spank someone for the first time? Talk so dirty even he himself can't believe what's coming out of his own mouth? Who cares? As long as you pull over first, put the top up if need be, and recline the seats for easier access, it doesn't matter how you get there. The question is, will you ever want to go home?

In 1962, GM, looking once again to shock the world through sheer performance, set in motion a run of Grand Sport Corvettes. The cars were tuned and tweaked to be so powerful that the front wheels could allegedly be lifted off the ground completely by stomping on the accelerator—in any gear. Sadly, the program stalled almost before it started and only a handful ever made their way from factories to showrooms. Just five remain in existence today.

Call it marketing genius or a colossal miscalculation, but the 1968 Hot Wheels Corvette somehow made its way to store shelves even before Chevrolet had unveiled the '68 model to car dealers. By the time it debuted, most, if not all, potential buyers (as well as competitors) knew exactly what it was going to look like. After all, their kids were already playing with a miniaturized version. To this day, the Corvette is still the most popular Hot Wheels car ever sold.

ON CAR SEX . . .

THE LOWDOWN
Because car culture is such a big part of modern civilization, many people have had—and continue to have—first-time sexual experiences in cars. So it's no wonder so many of us are excited by car sex!

TIPS AND TECHNIQUES
Keep your car sex *parked.* If it's the motion that turns you on, just do it while someone else is driving. Isn't that what backseats are for?

—Susan M. Block, Ph.D., author of
The 10 Commandments of Pleasure

AUTO EROTICA

My boyfriend owned an auto body shop, so I'd always take my car to him for repairs. I loved watching him work. Not only did he take a lot of pride in his job, he'd always get all hot and sweaty and wind up working in his tank top, all smudged with oil. One night we had plans for me to drop by the shop to pick up my car, and then we'd go for dinner. I went around back to find him, and there he was, giving my car one last wipe-down. He was in his oil-smudged tank top, a thin layer of sweat glistening on his skin. He smiled when he saw me, but I said nothing, choosing instead to grab him and kiss him, pulling him close to me as I leaned against the car. His breath was hot in my ear and I loved the musky scent of his skin, but the best part was when he bent me over the hood and had his way with me. The cool feel of the metal was a perfect balance for the heat of his body against mine. We never made it out to dinner, and my skirt was ruined with oil stains, but it was worth it! The skirt is actually still hanging in my closet as a remembrance of that hot night!

—Monique N., 28

"Except for the American woman, nothing interests the eye of the American man more than an automobile, or seems so important to him as an object of aesthetic appreciation."

Alfred Hamilton Barr, Jr.

✦ ✦ ✦ ✦

1965 *Ford Mustang*

It's not just an American automobile; it's *the* American automobile. Easily as red, white, and blue as apple pie, baseball at Yankee Stadium, or turkey and football on Thanksgiving Day, looking at the original ponycar calls to mind other great American pastimes—namely, doing the backstroke in the backseat, wandering hands on wandering highways, and poking around, after hours, in the undercarriage. The dazzling Ford Mustang not only ignited the senses, it combined all of the above in a sporty package that ran as wild as its namesake the second it was released, and cost just $2,368 to own.

The car was conceived with the full knowledge that by the mid-'60s, the largest population bubble in history was coming of age in America. Baby Boomers were about to rule, and it was little secret they had no interest in the cars their parents drove. The production Mustang was first shown to the public on April 17, 1964, inside the Ford Pavilion at the New York World's Fair. The unveiling was broadcast on all three (at the time) television networks. It went on sale at Ford dealers that same day, and within two years there were 1.5 million Mustangs on the road. It wasn't exotic. It also wasn't particularly fast (not with the inline six most people went for over the V8). And yet, compared to just about every other American car then in production, the Mustang was gorgeously sleek, a triumph in

styling, extraordinarily attractive—a car people were instantly passionate about. That passion carried from the showroom to the bedroom, albeit with a number of pit stops along the way.

You'd be hard-pressed to find someone older than forty who wasn't seduced by its expansive hood, long scallops, low-slug roof, and giant running-horse logo—or seduced in one, on one, or around one. Legend has it that babies conceived in Mustangs always come out male. Though that might not be true, few would argue that it isn't fun to try. Again and again and again if need be.

The prototype, first conceived by Ford product manager Donald N. Frey and championed by Ford division general manager Lee Iacocca, was a two-seat mid-engine roadster, but it was far too expensive. Something had to change, but what? Iacocca opened it up to a company-wide design contest. The resulting Ford Mustang we know and love today was actually envisioned by the Lincoln/Mercury design studio.

The Mustang made its debut with a price tag that read just about half as much as the Chevrolet Corvette. The initial advertisement read: "Presenting the Unexpected, Mustang has the look, the fire, the flavor of the great European car. Yet it's as American as its name . . . and as practical as its price." In the years since, there have been dozens of variations, model years, and restylings, some of them more dramatic than others. The only difference between the 1997 and 1998 Mustangs? The digital clock mounted on the instrument panel.

"When a man opens a car door for his wife, it's either a new car or a new wife."

Prince Philip

✦ ✦ ✦ ✦

ON CAR SEX . . .

THE LOWDOWN
The greatest allure of having sex in a car is the thrill of potentially being seen. Unless you suffer from claustrophobia, a feeling of being contained by a beautiful and strong machine while you are merging with your partner is quite exhilarating. And don't forget about having sex on top of the car—the warm car hood combined with cool air leads to a truly frisky experience!

TIPS AND TECHNIQUES
The only wrong way of having sex in the car is to do it while it is moving!

—Dr. Victoria Zdrok, "Dear Dr. Z" columnist for *Penthouse* magazine, and author of *Anatomy of Pleasure*

AUTO EROTICA

I never thought of myself as a car fanatic until the first time I had sex in one—that's when I learned to love leather and steel in a way that I'd never considered before. My college boyfriend loved his car so much that it was infectious—I couldn't help but get turned on when I was sitting in the passenger seat, watching his mounting glee as he took corners and playfully raced other drivers. I loved the way his hands gripped the steering wheel, the tensing of his jaw when he was concentrating on the road ahead. It was so hot.

So when I suggested a road trip, he was game. We had no idea where we were going—we just got in the car and started driving. But by the time we hit desert, I couldn't wait any longer, and suggested we pull off-road for a little nooky. There—in the sweltering heat, under a clear blue sky—I took him to the backseat and lifted up my skirt, straddling him, riding him until we were both drenched in sweat. I remember gripping the folds of the ragtop behind him to get leverage—almost like the car was a part of our experience. To this day it was one of the best sexual encounters of my life.

—Lisa W., 31

1966 *Ford Thunderbird*

What if you knew today was your last day on earth? What would you do? Where would you go? And perhaps more important, what would be your vehicle of choice to drive off into the sunset once and for all with that special someone at your side, your partner in crime? Obviously you'd want something stylish, fast, and luxurious. It probably wouldn't hurt if it was refined and comfortable, this being your final send-off before crossing the finish line. Only one car fits the bill. Car buffs know it. Collectors do, too. Thelma and Louise knew it as well; hell, they rode it to cinematic history. Meet the 1966 Thunderbird.

It started out simple enough, in 1955, as a two-seater designed for the young at heart. By the mid-'60s, it had grown into something far greater. Too big to be a sports car and faster than the typical sedan, it was America's answer to the "touring" and "saloon" cars of Europe. The decision was made to market it as a "personal luxury car." In addition to more seating, it gained an air scoop, a steering wheel that swung away for easy access, deeply sculpted flanks, an egg-crate grille, and a nose that came to a sharply chiseled, squared-off point. It was dignified, yet free-spirited, regal almost but with an undercoating of fun. It was ready to span time.

The Thunderbird begged passengers to take advantage. Once you'd pulled over, pushing the steering wheel to the side seemed the perfect way to invite her onto your lap. The wraparound dash provided added space and was perfect for her to brace herself against as her hips ground down into whoever was lucky enough to be in the seat. Even with the center console in place, the positions were endless and the low-slung roof, when it was up, meant those on the outside could sneak just a peek—enough to add a feeling of urgency, but not so much that the danger took over. Even if this wasn't your last day on earth, the T-Bird offered a glimpse of heaven few would soon forget.

The universe started out with a bang. Babies are conceived with a moan. As for the T-bird, the wheels were set in motion by one simple comment. Lewis D. Crusoe, a once-retired GM executive, and George Walker, a stylist, were ambling down a Parisian boulevard when Crusoe, spotting a sports car, wondered aloud, "Why can't we have something like that?" A simple phone call back to the plant settled the matter and work was begun almost instantly.

ON CAR SEX . . .

THE LOWDOWN
Cars are synonymous with freedom. Doing it in a car makes one feel wild, free, and very young again.

TIPS AND TECHNIQUES
The "right" or "wrong" way to have sex in a car depends entirely on where the car is parked—and how quickly you can steam up the windows!

—Susan Crain Bakos, author of *The Sex Bible*

Naming a car is never a simple affair, but in the case of the T-bird, it proved even more problematic than normal. Hep Cat, Beaver, Runabout, Arcturus, and El Tigre were all run up the flag pole, but none captured the car's spirit or potential buyers' imaginations. More important, all of them seemed to rub the brass the wrong way. In the end, the problem was solved with a company-wide contest: Whoever came up with a moniker worthy of the new vehicle would win an expensive suit. Stylist Alden Giberson was the victor. But Giberson, ever the practical one, asked for a $95 suit and an extra pair of trousers instead.

Though old cowboy imagery is responsible for many of today's car names (such as Cherokee, Pontiac, Bronco, and Mustang), "Thunderbird" actually comes from "Thunderbird Heights," a housing development in Rancho Mirage, California. Many a bet has been won bar-side with this simple piece of trivia.

AUTO EROTICA

I don't know what got into us—maybe it was the summer heat—but my girlfriend and I started playing a dirty little game of show-and-tell one night when I was driving her home. She'd hike up her skirt a little and give me a peek at what was underneath; I'd unbutton my shirt and show her a little of my broad chest. We kept teasing a little here and there until she really upped the ante by unbuttoning her blouse and flinging it open, daring me to do something. So I did. I pulled the car over to the curb—thank God it was a residential street—and helped her position herself sideways so that her head was resting against the door and her legs were over my shoulders. I kissed my way from her lips down her neck, across her perfect breasts, all the way down until I felt her buck her hips wildly into me. She still reminds me of that night every time we're in my car.

— Donnie F., 33

"I find it very difficult to draw a line between what's sex and what isn't. It can be very, very sexy to drive a car, and completely unsexy to flirt with someone at a bar."

Bjork

✦ ✦ ✦ ✦

1967 *Pontiac GTO*

Burnouts. Gasoline. Mayhem. This is what muscle cars are made of. And the GTO—loud, uncontrollable, and wild—was the car that set it all off.

While the hippies were tooling around in their Beetles and buses, this is the car real men blew past in. The kind of men who would fight for a woman. The kind of men who'd put it all on the line to prove a point. Mom and Dad knew better than to let their girls out of the house when a muscle car was on the prowl. But against better judgment, perhaps even because of the very idea of danger, the girls always go crazy for the bad boy.

From the very start, this car—and the men with balls big enough to make it growl— were rebels. While others cut weight to add speed, the GTO simply doubled up on the engine. After all, that's what real men did. The muscle beneath the hood was so pumped the car's stats had to be downplayed to make it past the Pontiac brass. But breaking the rules was the point. They worried it was too much. After all, they said, this was the era of "free love"—there weren't enough rule-breakers in the world to tame it, so they limited the first year production to just 5,000 cars. Two years later, that number had grown to more than 97,000. The times they were a-changin'.

The GTO was the brainchild of Pontiac engineer Russell Gee, an engine specialist, and Pontiac chief engineer John DeLorean. That's right, that DeLorean, of cocaine deals and *Back to the Future* fame.

Star of the movie *Triple X*, the GTO is a collector's piece the world over, but nowhere more so than in England, where muscle cars were never produced and are often too large for narrow London streets. There, the GTO, now a status symbol of conspicuous consumption among the elite, has been known to command prices upward of $250,000.

By the late '70s, though, words like "economy," "fuel efficiency," and "compact" had crept into the American lexicon, and production stopped for the GTO and others of its ilk. But as long as men still feel the need to take what they deserve and to fight for what they want—as long as there are still men who feel a discussion isn't always the best way to win an argument, and women still lust for the bad boy—the rebel spirit and the muscle cars that embodied it will live on. As for the rest, one press of the accelerator is all it takes to awaken the beast within.

AUTO EROTICA

I'll admit it—I got turned on every time I drove my first car. But nothing turned me on more than watching my girlfriend drive it. She was so aroused that she not only let me slip my hand under her skirt as she sped along, she took it and guided it to where she wanted it to go! I kissed her ear, nibbled her neck, and when I brought her to orgasm, she nearly drove us off the road. But instead of driving us back to campus so we could finish what we started in the bedroom, she pulled in front of the building I lived in. We jumped in the backseat, with me feverishly undoing my belt and pants and her pulling up her skirt for easier access. It was a night we'll never forget . . . and I wound up giving her my spare set of keys.

—Shawn P., 30

"*Recycling and speed limits are bullshit; they're like someone who quits smoking on his deathbed.*"

Chuck Palahniuk

✦ ✦ ✦ ✦

ON CAR SEX . . .

THE LOWDOWN
Cars themselves are erotic, all that hot metal rumbling beneath you. Then there's the sudden ecstasy of a spontaneous moment when you reach over and grab your lover. It's sex on wheels, baby!

TIPS AND TECHNIQUES
Right way: getting off in the driver's seat. Wrong way: getting caught!

—Laura Corn, author of
101 Nights of Grrreat Sex

1969 *Chevrolet El Camino*

Business in the front. Party in the back. It takes a certain kind of man to rock the look. You see, while some guys will pay well above ticket price to take a woman to the concert, others are content bringing the party to the parking lot. One part muscle car, one part pickup, the El Camino is, was, and always will be the undisputed king of the tailgate. A car for boys who don't see the point of imported beer—why pay so much when PBR cans are priced to move?—the guys who want to rock and roll all night and party every day, and the girls who ride along with them, line up at the backstage door looking for a pass. That's the story with the Super Sport (the SS model, pictured), anyway.

It all starts in 1957 with the Ford Ranchero. A boxy, hybrid car/truck that had all the sex appeal of a root canal, few people really thought it would find a market. Yet in its first year alone, Ford moved a staggering 22,246 units. Chevrolet, trying to play catch-up, stuck a truck bed on the already popular Impala and rushed it to showrooms. But where the Ranchero had been utilitarian—the Swiss Army knife of cars for buyers who wanted the best of both worlds—the Impala was a little too classy to be used in the same way, and just two years in, the model was pulled.

Following a three-year absence, Chevy came back using the Chevelle/Malibu for the front end, and guess what: It was an instant smash! A beefed-up, tough-guy workhouse pulling a pickup, but able to corner. What could be more manly? And in 1968, when Chevy offered the car with the Super Sport package, a drag racer's delight, what was a good idea suddenly became a classic, a diamond in the rough to be cherished for generations to come.

Fancier than a truck, more useful than a passenger car, able to leap past sports cars in a single bound, and better looking than just about anything else on the road, the El Camino filled a need few even knew they had. It found sex appeal in a place few knew it existed. It took it from the speedway to the tattoo shop to the showroom to the rock show—and it did it a with a swagger, an attitude, and a look that few could resist. Those who tried to, men anyway, sometimes went home alone, while their ladies hung around for the after-party. It was just that kind of ride.

AUTO EROTICA

When my boyfriend and I went camping, we really roughed it—we didn't even take a tent, choosing instead to sleep out under the stars. I was finally able to convince him to at least take air mattresses with us to lie down in the flatbed of his truck, which fit our sleeping bags perfectly. Our first night out, we set up our sleeping bags and pillows and got a fire roaring, and then cuddled up under the covers, spooning to keep warm. But we were still cold, so we decided to take it a step further. Nibbling my ear, my boyfriend slipped his hand between my legs and started teasing me with his fingers. When I couldn't take it anymore, I flipped him over and slid on top of him, my hands planted on the truck's rear window. A couple of fellow campers passed by us while we were in the throes of passion, but we didn't care—having them see us was part of the fun!

—Carolee A., 24

ON CAR SEX . . .

THE LOWDOWN
Hmm, I've only done it twice in the thirty years I've been sexually active, so . . . privacy, potential for great scenery, the kink/nostalgia factor, and, perhaps, the "naughty" factor are the allures of having sex in a car.

TIPS AND TECHNIQUES
I'd think the backseat would be a little more roomy and less uncomfortable than the front seat, especially if the car has bucket seats . . . Avoid public places. Avoid the gear shift.

—Nina Hartley, nurse, swinger, and sexual adventurer

"Power is the ultimate aphrodisiac."

Henry Kissinger

◆ ◆ ◆ ◆

1970 *Jaguar E-Type*

To the slender mods, the form-fitted Twiggies, and London's scenesters, Jaguar's E-Type was an aphrodisiac like no other. Where one might expect to find a grille instead was what appeared to be a tiny mouth, lips parted ever so slightly. The headlights, round, voluptuous, and framed in giant, chrome ovals, called to mind a woman wearing thick eyeliner and an unblinking, come-hither stare. Its expansive never-ending hood featured a suggestive bulge, and just enough metal to cover its lanky V12 engine. Is it any surprise that Austin Powers dubbed his the "Shaguar"?

Sensual and seductive in design and overflowing with unashamed showmanship, the E-Type represents everything that was fast, cool, and sexy about the '60s. It revolutionized sports car design. The 150-mph top speed was devastatingly quick. A fully independent suspension and power-assisted disc brakes gave it a limousine-like ride. It had a vicelike grip on the road despite slender tires that looked better suited to a bike than a world-class racer. And, at nearly one-third the price of the Aston Martin DB4, it was perhaps Britain's greatest bargain.

As a result, car lovers the world over were forced to ask some pretty tough questions. Mainly, when is a car not just a car, but rather a work of art? And with so much sex appeal,

shouldn't there be more room to, er, stretch out? As pop stars, race car drivers, and royalty jostled for position on an ever-lengthening waiting list for delivery, it was New York City's Museum of Modern Art (MOMA) that answered the first question by acquiring one for its permanent collection in 1996. As for the second question, concerning room, Jaguar was eventually forced to add a backseat. Not only did this addition enable more than one passenger to come along for the ride, but it took advantage of the car's sex appeal for steamy backseat encounters. Don't forget—it was the swinging '60s!

The original choice of car for James Bond in the movie *Goldfinger* was an E-Type. Unfortunately, Jaguar, which was already having trouble keeping up with demand, was forced to pass, just as it had to do with the TV show *The Saint* in the months that followed. Instead, Bond was pushed into an Aston Martin DB5. Following the movie's release, sales increased by nearly fifty percent for the DB5.

AUTO EROTICA

I had been traveling a lot for business, and my girlfriend and I really missed each other. So when I was back in the office one Monday around lunchtime, I called my girlfriend at home and asked her if she'd come meet me. She was game—and even showed up wearing a skirt with no panties! She hopped in my car and we drove around looking for a spot to be alone, finally settling on an alleyway behind an office complex. She leaned her seat all the way back and I climbed over the center console. Propping one foot on the dashboard and the other on the console, she hiked up her skirt and guided my hands up her thighs as she kissed me. It was hard to navigate both of us in the passenger seat, but somehow the challenge made it more intimate—more connected. We nearly got caught a couple of times when someone drove past, but we were able to effectively play it off. I drove her back to her car and went back to work with a smile on my face.

—Daniel M., 36

ON CAR SEX . . .

THE LOWDOWN
Many people have an exhibitionistic streak but are scared to fully indulge it. Being in a car gives the "we might be caught" thrill without the same level of danger as having sex in public.

TIPS AND TECHNIQUES
Doing it in a position that could knock the handbrake off and send you rolling down a hill is about as bad as you can get. It's also worth going for "discreet" positions such as missionary so that, if anyone comes along, you're mostly covered up, rather than, say, doggie where you'll be exposed for anyone to see.

—Emily Dubberley, founder of cliterati.co.uk and author of *Brief Encounters*

"It is not enough to conquer; one must know how to seduce."

Voltaire

♦ ♦ ♦ ♦

1971 *Dodge Challenger*

Power is sexy. So are strength and muscle. What's even sexier, though, is the confidence to know you've got both, without the need or desire to flaunt it. It's the guy who tries to talk his way out of a fight, only to win, hands down, when pushed beyond the point of diplomacy. Superman hiding beneath Clark Kent's glasses. That was the attitude the Dodge Challenger brought with it when it first rolled off the assembly line in 1970. It took the world a while to realize exactly what it was dealing with, but once it did, the Challenger, a late-entry answer to Ford's Mustang, would be one of the most collectible cars in history.

Built using the Plymouth Barracuda platform, the two-door Challenger's styling was simple; the looks, subdued. In fact, with the possible exception of the optional shaker hood (shown), there was little to suggest the car was remarkable in any way. But it *was* remarkable, for pinned beneath the unassuming hood was perhaps the largest Hemi (an engine in which the internal combustion chambers are hemispherical, making it more efficient and powerful) stitched into any production automobile at the time

Some men make threats, saying things like, "Do you know who I am?" Others let their adversaries find out the hard way. Which do women go for? Take the expression, "His bark is worse than his bite." This car never let out a peep, but once it sunk its teeth in, those lucky

enough to experience its full force were forever marked. Doggy-style, a super-hero; anyway way you cut it, this was no two-pump chump. Its irregular pistons hit the spot, fast and hard, with more than enough thrust to leave its name on their lips for years to come.

Though the 1970 and 1971 Dodge Challenger remain favorites of enthusiasts, by 1972, as government regulations tightened, the Challenger had lost its characteristic Hemi. With a less powerful engine, it took almost nine seconds to reach forty mph. Also gone was the convertible option. Following the '74 model year, Dodge discontinued the line completely.

The car made famous by the 1971 movie *Vanishing Point* (a film that centers around a bet that a car can't be driven from Denver to San Francisco in just fifteen hours) was far from a casting afterthought; the movie itself never would have been made were it not for the vehicle it featured. Director Richard C. Sarafian was approached on behalf of the Chrysler Corporation with a simple, yet pragmatic question: Can you make a movie from a car? The answer: Why not? The muscle car craze was in full swing and bigger blockbusters had been built around thinner premises. With this in mind, the writers pounded out the screenplay. Of the eight brand-new 1970 Challengers given for the film's production, seven were completely totaled while the eighth was actually stolen. Interestingly, not all eight (featured in the movie as just one) were originally the off-white they appear to be on screen. Several had to be painted to match. For this reason, discerning viewers will notice an underlying green hue from the car's original paint when it is scratched, dinged, or dented.

AUTO EROTICA

I had taken my car on a pretty rugged road trip with the boys, so when my girlfriend saw how dirty the car was—and how exhausted I was—she graciously offered to wash it. When I walked into the backyard, I stopped dead in my tracks: She was wearing a little pair of teeny, tiny cutoff shorts, a cut-up white T-shirt, and no bra. Did I mention she was soaking wet? She knew I was watching her, so she made sure to get extra soapy and made a big production of leaning across the car, her bottom peeking out from her skimpy shorts. After watching her sexy show for a few minutes, I had about all I could take. I ripped off her shorts, leaned her against the car, and pulled her legs around my waist. The car rocked against us with our every move; it was hard to hang on to her with how wet she was, not to mention how slick the car was. But she felt amazing! I've never looked at a car wash the same way since.

—Hunter R., 30

"To attract men, I wear a perfume called New Car Interior."

Rita Rudner

✦ ✦ ✦ ✦

2004 *Ferrari 360 Modena*

The lines are sleek. The curves tight. The side intakes, designed to gulp air as the vehicle rockets up the motorway, dramatic. And the engine, encased in glass like the work of art it is, looks more like something you'd find on an aircraft carrier than on the highway. But all that is for the gawker passing the incredible Ferrari 360 Modena on the street. You, the driver, have something far more exciting in store.

The interior reveals a series of aesthetic features designed to inspire the senses. Here, leather and aluminum combine in an exhilarating show of Italian perfection. Swooping custom-tailored seats caress your every contour as you admire the cluster of gauges, the padded dash, and the fine hand-wrought detailing.

A simple twist of the key, though, and all that serenity is lost. The engine, located just inches behind your right ear, erupts with an impatient whine as the 400 horses spring to life, fulfilling their destiny. The warmth of the steering wheel is interrupted by the cold metal F1 electrohydraulic shift paddles hidden behind it. The smell of hot oil makes its way from the glazed-in V8, and all that leather is helpless as your nostrils sample the first hint of the Ferrari legacy: Stripped-down performance hidden beneath a thick veil of luxury.

It's rare that one is aware of the very instant fantasy becomes reality, but as you prepare to press the accelerator for the first time, you will experience just such a moment. A single heartbeat later and you're shooting up the tarmac at sixty miles per hour, quickly approaching the 185-mile-per-hour peak. You become a blur to those you overtake, an object of envy. From the cockpit, the dotted line in the road becomes a single, hardened beam. From the passenger's seat, you look like a hero. Your heart pounds in your ears. Most men would kill for a ride like this. Most women would die for a man like you. Instinct takes over as you, she, and this machine intertwine. Few people ever have this type of threesome.

Customers laying out $250,000-plus for a Ferrari are treated exceptionally well. They're invited to the factory to pick out colors, fabrics, and leather styles. They get to tour the assembly line. They can also accept personal delivery of their new baby right there in Maranello, just a short drive south of Modena, in north-central Italy, if they so choose. Before accepting the keys, though, they're asked to sign the factory wall. There, signatures go up alongside those of Jay Leno, Ralph Lauren, and Wyclef Jean, among others.

Ferrari knows the impact a role in a major motion picture can have. The company loaned one out so that James Bond could race against it in *Goldeneye*. Bond was set to win, but while filming the scene, there was an accident. As a result, and because the crew couldn't afford to pay for the damage, the script was changed so that the Ferrari, not Bond's Aston Martin, took the checkered flag.

AUTO EROTICA

When you've spent the evening teasing the love of your life, sometimes making it all the way back to the bedroom takes way too long. I'd been at a work function with my boyfriend and spent the evening whispering sweet-and-sexy nothings in his ear, subtly detailing things I was going to do to him when we got home while sneakily touching him places to let him know how serious I was. On the drive home, I turned up the heat, as did he—both of us were telling the other exactly how it was going to go down once we made it back in the house, except we never did make it back! By the time our garage door was halfway down, I was on top of him in the driver's seat, kissing him and licking his neck as he feverishly undid my top. Realizing we weren't going to have any room inside the car, I pushed the door open and climbed off him, peeling off my pants and hopping up on the hood. He met me there and entered me slowly, loving me tenderly but passionately. We were so exhausted when we were done that we almost fell asleep on the car, until we realized the garage door still hadn't closed all the way, letting in a mighty draft—as well as entertaining any passersby!

—Becky W., 28

"What makes the engine go?
Desire, desire, desire."

Stanley Kunitz

♦ ♦ ♦ ♦

ON CAR SEX . . .

THE LOWDOWN
Sex in cars is spontaneous and heated—you never actually plan to do it; it just happens because you want someone so badly that you just can't wait. It's raw and it's real, which means fumbling around a little is okay.

TIPS AND TECHNIQUES
Make sure you ease the seat back so your ass doesn't hit the wheel over and over again; straddling is always the best position to begin with when you pull over for some fun. Roll the windows up and keep them up no matter what: the steam may be a sign of amour to passersby, but it will give you more privacy.

—Lainie Speiser, publicist for *Penthouse* magazine

2006 *Lotus Elise*

The seats are cramped. The pedals feel like mousetraps. The engine, a Toyota-built, 1.8-liter, four-cylinder, generates just 190 horsepower. And yet no car is, or has ever been, more fun to drive. Young boys play with Matchbox, Tonka, and go-karts. Grown men get similar kicks from the $40,000 Lotus Elise. Women go for the young at heart.

At 1,500 pounds, the Elise's weight is just over half that of the similarly proportioned Porsche Boxter. But with weight cut so severely—the car was chopped down to just a tiny fiberglass body, aluminum frame, and an engine—these candy-coated monsters achieve extreme performance in spite of their relatively modest power output. Sometimes bigger *isn't* better.

What would it be like to ride a roller coaster off its rails? Climb into the driver's seat and find out. Want to save your dream girl from the mundane? Steal her away to a life less ordinary? Invite her along for the ride.

The engine starts with the push of a button. Let her do the honors. Twist the wheel into the first tightly wound turn and the adrenaline hits. Take it with a woman at your side.

Your hearts pound as the tachometer throbs towards the red line. Your palms sweat. Faces go flush. The blood heads south. Within seconds the speedometer crosses the

ON CAR SEX . . .

THE LOWDOWN

It's difficult to explain our attraction to automobile sex, other than the fact it takes us back to our teen years, when bedrooms were scarce and opportunities to satisfy our raging libidos were few and far between.

TIPS AND TECHNIQUES

Sure, the transmission knob or steering wheel could make things a tad uncomfortable, but it's a small price to pay for orgasmic release. After all, there's no right or wrong way to do it in a car—just a way.

—Ian and Alicia Denchasy (aka Freddy and Eddy), sex writers and store owners, Freddy and Eddy—Where Couples Can Come

"Speed provides the one genuinely modern pleasure."

Aldous Huxley

◆ ◆ ◆ ◆

100-mph mark. Within minutes she'll be in your arms. Within hours she'll be bragging to friends. And within days you'll be flooring it to the next adventure. Together. After all, it's hard to have this much fun without a playmate. Even for adults.

First conceived in early 1994, the Elise roadster—so named for then Lotus chairman Romano Artioli's granddaughter Elisa—wasn't released by English manufacturer Lotus Cars until 1996.

Many current Lotus owners owe their passion to the James Bond series. It is the fulfillment of a childhood dream that started the second Bond drove that beautiful white Esprit into the water in *The Spy Who Loved Me*. It made a second appearance in *For Your Eyes Only*, but the automaker's next starring role wasn't until Richard Gere picked up a streetwalking Julia Roberts in *Pretty Woman*.

Just how important can movie placement be to an automotive manufacturer? After the release of *The Spy Who Loved Me*, demand for white Lotus Esprits reached such a point that prospective customers were put on a three-year waiting list by Lotus Cars.

AUTO EROTICA

My boyfriend and I share a love of luxury and speed, so sometimes, just for kicks, we would test-drive cars we had no hope of affording. Usually the car salesmen wanted to go with us, but one day we happened upon one who was lazy and let us take a sporty two-seater out by ourselves. We sped off into the afternoon sun, leaving the top down so the wind could whip through our hair. After driving a few miles, my boyfriend got this look in his eye suggesting he wanted something more. We drove to a nearby park and found a secluded parking spot. He asked me to stand up, so I did—grabbing on to the windshield frame to steady myself—and he pushed my legs apart, leaving one on my seat, and positioning the other on his as he maneuvered underneath me. He removed my panties, then slowly brushed his tongue from my ankle to my knee, up my thigh, all the way up my skirt. His strokes encircled me, making me shake and quiver so much I thought I was going to lose my balance. It didn't take me long to climax, and by the time I finished quaking, we had to return the car. However, I quickly repaid the favor when we got home!

—Christina M., 29

Index

PRIVATE PARKING
UNAUTHORIZED OR ILLEGALLY PARKED VEHICLES WILL BE IMPOUNDED
CUSTOMER PARKING WHILE PATRONIZING ONLY
NO OVERNIGHT PARKING
MVP TOW (213) 251-8937
CALIFORNIA
X 1958 X